Human Frequencies

Children of the Light – I looked through my window

Milton DeWayne Benson

Copyright © 2010 by Milton DeWayne Benson
First Edition – June 2010

www.dropdeadhappy.com
Thank you Mark K. for your support, insight and providing a welcome home to my articles on personal growth and self-acceptance

ISBN
978-1-77067-100-3 (Hardcover)
978-1-77067-101-0 (Paperback)
978-1-77067-102-7 (eBook)

All rights reserved.

No part of this publication may be reproduced in any form, or by any means, electronic or mechanical, including photocopying, recording, or any information browsing, storage, or retrieval system, without permission in writing from the publisher.

Photo on Cover
Enchanted Forrest – The Ancient Hump-backed Stone Warrior
took a boulder as his seat
Into the leaves of the Desert Willow the Black Cat,
Green Snake and Brown Fox did leap
Waiting as the waters of time cross the hand of fate
Into to the fog of eternity it falls away as they wait

Published by:

FriesenPress
Suite 300 – 777 Fort Street
Victoria, BC, Canada V8W 1G9

www.friesenpress.com

For information on bulk orders contact:
info@friesenpress.com or fax 1-888-376-7026

Distributed to the trade by The Ingram Book Company

Table of Contents

— **Preface** — vii
— **Forward** — ix
— **Acknowledgements** — xi

The State of Life 1
Children of the Light................................3
Twilight is Calling 4
To Those I Have Loved, And Those Whom Have Loved Me...5
Touched By The Sun 6
To React 6
The Winds of Change 7
Timeless..7
The Gods of Greed 8
The Veil 8

Twilight is Calling 9
The blank page 12
The Attitude of Gratitude (Thank You Job) 12
Sometimes..13
I do not seek pity 14
My Greatest Addiction 14
Eileen 15
Michelle..16

The Plight of Man..................................17
My Plight (my wild horses)..........................19
I Cannot Say..20
Spend..20
Had I Only Known 21
A String of Pearls 22

Tiny Bubbles.......................................23
For Today and Tomorrow 25
Equanimity 26
Creatures of Habit 26
Doing Nothing 27
Beyond the Past 27

Evolution...29
Evolution..30
Break the Mold......................................30
Beloved Sister 31

Along the Road..32
Answers 33
Addictions Wings 34

The Path of Least Resistance........................35
Be Divine...37
I Cannot Change 38
If I could choose....................................39
The View 39

Because I Love You................................41
Because I love you 43
Child of today.......................................43
The Muse...44
It was You 44
Now life is brighter still 45
I cannot complain 46
The Shape Shifter 47

Fractured 49
True Love...51
Deja Vu 51
The Ship..52
Love's Toll 53
Your Memory Torments Me.........................53
Where lies your power?..............................54
It's a New Day 55
Those Echoes of Childhood 55

Society 57
Maybe it's just me 59
Open the Windows 60
Perfectly Imperfect 61

Primordial Waters 63
Scatter the Ashes....................................65
Razors Edge 66
The Darkness.......................................67
The pace quickening 68

Desert(ed) River...................................69
Till I no longer breathe 71
No comfort in comfort 72
Stagnant Rain Drops 73

From the Heights **75**
My Hope 77

Hope Falls **79**
Web Articles and Presentations published at DropDead-
Happy.com. 81

Possibilities **87**
I'm Bored !!! 89
Who is driving the bus? 90
Don't Forget to Breathe 91

Foot Steps **95**
The Aggravation of Expectation. 97
The Winds of Change 98
The Banquet 98

Hard Water **99**
In That Light 101
Keep The Bridges 101
The Smile. 102
Fighting the Power (of Expectation) 103
The Silence Song. 104

Survival of the Fittest. **105**
Scatter The Ashes 106
The Fly 107
Facing the AIDS virus head on. By Stephanie Frith 108
POZitively Speaking 110
The Presentation. 110

The Death of an Era **113**
P.S. Make Me Laugh. 115
Comedy Bio. 120

— Epilogue — **121**

I looked through My Window **122**

— Preface —

Perhaps it isn't the events in life that define us.
Perhaps it is what we do because of, or in spite of, those events that colors who we truly are.
Perhaps we won't be judged by what we do but instead because of why we did it.
Perhaps we could blame everyone else for our life or just move forward and make it our life.
Perhaps we aren't as smart as we believe and in fact are just lucky.
Perhaps it's not about change but learning to accept the loss and growth that comes.
Perhaps it's not about giving away our power but accepting it as our own.
Perhaps true forgiveness starts not with others but ourselves.
Perhaps the greatest love suffers when its enemy suffers.
And perhaps it rejoices whenever anyone rejoices.
Perhaps its not a choice of good or bad but of faith and devotion.
Perhaps in giving we truly receive more.
Perhaps prayer isn't designed for our will, praise or needs.
Perhaps no one will ever read this book but perhaps the one person who needs it will find it.
Perhaps God is more loving, kind, generous and forgiving than we realize.
Perhaps Jesus, Yeshua, is more than prophets like Mohammed, Elijah, Isaiah or Buddha, or perhaps they are all roads to God.
Perhaps there is nothing after this life perhaps I choose to hedge my bets.
Perhaps my polluted life, mind and spirit can find joy and blessings in this life's challenges.
Perhaps I am asleep and this is all just a dream.
Perhaps I'll find heaven in creation today.

— Forward —

No matter what you may think of this collection I consider life blessed and there are no true miracles in life until I realized that life itself was a miracle. I feel this way about any creative gift people express because this unique "Voice" is theirs and theirs alone and that is a miraculous thing to behold.

Still almost every artist works to perfect their work yet when that Divine Spark of Inspiration hits me the words just seem to fall from my pen.

Where come the words from my pen,
If not to capture to lose again
Falling into place without fighting
Striking me as if lightening

In my defense I am diagnosed with Bipolar Affective Disorder, have lived with HIV since the 1980's, have been on chemotherapy to save my liver from Hepatitis C.

But, for me, it's not about the challenges.

Still, I often wonder how I can live with the Manic-Depression, aka. Bipolar Affective Disorder (or B.A.D.) Social Anxiety Disorder (or S.A.D.) and Reactive Attachment Disorder (or R.A.D.) and still deal with the world outside my brain. The following are just thoughts captured during those moments I felt that Divine Inspiration and Manic Creation.

— Acknowledgements —

OMG- where to begin? I am thankful for a life which has given me challenges which I have not only survived but overcome and used as seeds for a more beautiful life – even if only just in my head.

I am thankful for the Family I have now even more than before.

I am thankful that even though I do not have everything I want I have always had everything I needed.

I am thankful that I do not look at what I do not have because then I would have nothing.

I am thankful for Family and Faith even if each may seem lacking at one point they never stop amazing me.

I am thankful for the suffering of Yeshua, Jesus, Christ who suffered more than I shall ever have to experience

I am thankful to Buddha who thought enough to share Mind Fullness, Impermanence and Attachment

I am thankful to my Heavenly Father and my Earthly Mother without either I am nothing

I am thankful for my dark days because the bright ones are even brighter

I am thankful that one day I will die because there will be no more physical, mental and spiritual suffering that I see within myself and within most others

I am especially thankful for this chance to share this with you!

The State of Life

I selected this first piece dedicated to my sister Kimberlye. It came to me in less than 5 minutes on 2/14/06 within 10 minutes of hearing of her stem-cell transplant had failed and her Leukemia was once again in charge. On some levels this is a small part of my faith system. But this poem wasn't written to justify any specific Faith or Belief System but to express some type of continuity between life and death. To express the Life Force, Chi, Spirit or Soul. This poem was created to comfort her. I had hoped to share with her in person but instead shared it for the 1st time at her memorial service.

Children of the Light

Sweet Child of Light
You are born of stardust
Living in a fragment… Living in a moment
Not to expire but to change….. As all energy never dies
That vibration in the smallest molecular level
Is the energy in everything even the star dust
Dust which fed the primordial stew of earthly existence
And continues on in each of us
Children of light
soon you shall shed the halo
the coil of mortality
the frail limited body must go
Children of light
that vibration inside
will not cease but continue to thrive
born from beyond time limited no longer by ties that bind
Oh Child of Light
fear not the signs
for this life is but a moment by design
Children of the Light
do not fear the eventual change
as you must move forward
from this confining space
Oh Sweet Child of Light
there is no other way
To be welcomed back into the warmth
from which life began
As Children of the Light
We shall all meet again
Bound by the very stardust,
Energy and vibration of the cosmos
Never to have to say good bye again
Good Bye, Sweet Child of the Light
In a moment I too will be at your side

To me the sentiment in "Twilight is Calling- (Crying is for the Dead)" is much stronger than the actual structure in the poem. It is a lasting memory and gift from my Grandfather and namesake Milton Krell.

Twilight is Calling
(Crying is for the Dead)

At one time I was the apple of his eye
But in a moment in the hospital he lie
I just 6, entered, and could only cry
He had changed so much since the last time

Twilight was calling his name

Mine being the same
Yet, I didn't know what to say
He turned his head a tear in his eye
And chuckled to choke back his cry

"Tears are for the Dead" he replied

And he turned his head back with no more word to speak
His words and actions were the last I would know
Till his funeral where the cries did grow
He left me with a legacy I didn't quite understand

Still I tried to live by it as best I could plan

Everyday a new meaning comes to hand
That life is meant for the living and crying for the end.
When twilight is calling and I am on my death bed
I will laugh and with a tear in my eye, chuckle and turn my head

Laughter is for the living, crying is for the dead

I cannot claim authorship on this poem only editing and revision adding a few lines to a card that had crossed my path before David, my partner and love of 17 years. I read this at his memorial service 5/2001

To Those I Have Loved
And Those Whom Have Loved Me

When i am gone
Release me and let me go
I have a new world to know.
Do not tie yourself to me with tears
Be happy for all of our years.

I gave you my love my very best
You gave me joy and happiness.
You each have given, and our love has grown
And in that we will never be alone.

So grieve for me if you must
But find comfort in the memories of us.
It is only a short time we will be apart
Bless and share those memories
Still living in your heart.
Life will go on
So remember i won't be far away.
When you need me at your side i will stay.
Though you cannot see or touch me
I will be near.

Just listen with your heart
And you will feel and hear
My love
So soft and ever clear.

And when the time comes
That you must walk this same road
I will be here waiting
To welcome you home

Touched By The Sun

Oh to feel that gentle caress
To feel that loving pressure upon my skin
The weight of a million particles of energy that touch within
Reaching into my soul, my very depth

The power to feed a world of creatures in need of the light
A light of warmth and strength is given without requite
Who can deny the power felt even without the ability of sight
To help draw a seed from the dark
Essential to life does the sun energies impart
Touching caressing me even when I am dark

A sun who's power should never be forgotten
An essential element for this life we have trodden
To savor the particles reigning down upon me
Is to come as close to creation as I can be
To feel it's weight pushing me down along with gravity
In it's light I grow freely

To React

Nature takes its course
I can only react
Life moves with force
I can only react
My thoughts follow their own course
I can only react
Come shame, pain and remorse
I can only react
Come ecstasy, joyful discourse
I can only react
As a ship tossed upon the sea
I can only react
Or on glass a calm as can be
I can only react
Helpless I feel I can only react
If I could make my sails a new tack
To blow a new wind toward the mast
Then I would do more than react

The Winds of Change

The Winds of Change envelop me
Drive me to places and times I cannot tell
Force me into unseen times as well
The Winds of Change buffet me
Pushing me onward
Onward through Eternity
The Winds of Change become Me
As I relent to their ferocity
The Winds of Change move me
I have no choice floating on Life's Sea
Than to hope to navigate the unseen
The Winds of Change that be

Timeless

Candles extinguished
Clock stopped
Breath ceases
Now the eternal clock

Tears fall
Memories shared
Lonely moments
Grief must not stop

Companion lost
Love must progress
Empty days
Thoughts digress

A moment of ease
Eventually three
Something stirs
Smiles progress

Heart still beats
A warm reminisce
Repetitive this
Timeless till the end

The Gods of Greed

Pinnacles rise calling their name
Letters on an index they became
At one time ethics reigned
The slaves had value in some past day
Cast aside no longer having a place till his grave
The God's finding cheaper more willing slaves
More riches for them to plunder
Gold for them to save
A new land to take
Humanity they forsake
The God's of Greed always thunder
That is not their fault that mankind suffer
That any man can be a God of Greed
Provided he serves only his own need
And use the slaves for what they be
Pawns in chess game
Played by the God's of Greed.

The Veil

A thin line between the real and surreal
A voice expressing how you should feel
Choices and opinions leak out
Fantasy and reality comes each shout
Life it is sometimes about
A glow, an ember pure
Leaving impressions I am sure
Of things that are and cannot be
On the veil it can be seen
Light ever changing upon the scene
The veil captures all who see
All those looking upon that screen
Entranced by pictures and knowledge there be
Often lost in a moment of comedy
Lost in the veil of the T.V.
A veil that separates from action and activity
To feed the mind with mindful and mindless things
The veil tears me from my reality
And blinds me from the life meant for me.

Twilight is Calling

The Planted Seed

We often plant seeds of relationship
So often expecting it to grow into that or this
Often attached to ones need for harmonious bliss
Blinded by the outcome the red flags are missed
Trying to create something that wasn't meant to exist
One cannot force a turnip to be a tulip
Every relationship is like the planted seed
But no one knows the genus, species or breed
Each must endeavor to nurture, water the seed
And discover what grows up so freely
A seed as precious as any relationship it can grow
But what it is requires time and effort you know
Do not expect it to be a melon, pear or weed
Because it might become a pumpkin, flower or tree
And to expect any more is simply insanity
To think one can force it to become something it is not
Is to feed instead disappointment, sorrow on the lot
Give the seed water and time to grow
Patiently waiting for it's true nature to show
Perhaps a friend or more it will grow to be
Still One cannot change the nature of that planted seed
Nor can it be changed by want, desire or need
Because it will be what it will be
So plant your seeds and tend with care
To discover the possibilities that are there
And don't be disappointed if your expectations aren't met
Because relationships, like seeds, should have no regrets
They strive to grow upward into the light
Following their nature each seed possesses its own life
Each relationship and seed grows by its own design
So don't label, box or pull it before you recognize
What it is that you see before your eyes.

The blank page

The blank page
screams to be heard
waiting for a hand to caress a word
to touch and permeate it's being
and echo the sentiment it is feeling
Few words can have as much meaning
many words can also be deceiving
The page, the palette, the creation unveiling
the page lives while words assail it
to breathe the life and sing the song
of the words that tattoo it however long
and show the soul from which it was born
The blank page sits and screams for more.

The Attitude of Gratitude (Thank You Job)

I've been hearing a lot of people saying
"You need an Attitude of Gratitude"
Still this seems to be coming from those
who live in an "Attitude for Platitudes'
Espousing things like
"Don't worry, Be happy"
Sorry I live in the real world
I cannot ascribe to repeating things so sweet and sappy
No, simple sayings can become a wicked crutch
And only have value when said in faith and trust
A simple saying cannot sway my reality
So I look instead at what has been given me
So many look for miracles in this life
When in fact the miracle is to be alive in this time
I count what I have now and let go what has been lost
In gratitude I count my blessings today and not their cost
And many days I suffer like Job
Who suffered the loss of everything he once could hold
His family, his lands, his wealth and health taken away
He suffered pain every day
But he claimed to have been blessed
To live life in this hard way
To have had everything and then it was gone
Still he had the Attitude of Gratitude that couldn't go wrong
And perhaps I have suffered a little of his lot
But it could have always have been worse,
Could it not???

Sometimes

Sometimes I want to confront my family with the truth
To stand up and say what seemed so egregious all those years ago
Sometimes I want to disavow any knowledge of their existence
And say what happened was just a fantasy
Sometimes I just want them to apologize
Although that would not change a thing
Sometimes I just hope they would be fair and decent
But I realize that isn't their nature
Sometimes I wish they could spend a day in my shoes
And walk through the memories and thoughts of my mind
Sometimes I wish life wasn't such a struggle
But even the smallest seed struggles to grow
Sometimes I wish it was all different
But then I would not be the same either
Sometimes I just want to be someone else
But that only makes my issues seem worse
Sometimes I want to be as big and expanse as the universe
Lost in worlds untold only to have life unfold and draw me back into its gravity
Sometimes I just want it all to feel right
So I let it go and travel into my light
Sometimes I step out of the box I have walled myself in
Only to find myself hiding behind those walls again
Sometimes I want to scream and yell the truth
But who would listen? Who would listen?
Sometimes I admit that the future is brighter than the past
The unknown calls me to move at last
Sometimes those days haunt my every step
But I keep trudging away my very best
Yet sometimes I know that life is good
Feeling it deep within my very soul
Sometimes life is beyond compare
I have moved beyond the days of despair
Sometimes I only want to fight
But with life and thoughts that do not seem right
Sometimes it seems a holy battle
Well worth the efforts and the travails
Sometimes I admit these are better days
more often that not I give praise
Because everything seems better than my past
I step out of its shadow at last
Sometimes

I do not seek pity
(semi-finalist in Immortal Voices at Poetry.com 1./27/07)

You cannot know the depths and darkness I have seen
You do not know that challenges there have been
You do not know the heights of insanity I've seen
You do not know the road I've walked
You do not know how others talked
You do not know the shame I've hawked
I do not know what I have lost
I only know the paths I've had to cross
I do not seek pity
I bear it with humility
I wear it only within me
Others I cannot or will not envy
I face it alone
I do not seek pity
In the end everyone faces it alone
I laugh but have no pity
It was just meant to be

My Greatest Addiction

I cannot say what is my greatest addiction
Perhaps it is waking up addicted to air
And I cannot say what my greatest addiction does
Perhaps it is like the caffeine in the tea I prepare
I cannot say how my addiction came to be
Like Faith or Hope clinging in that air I breathe
I do not know why I feel as an addict
I no longer participate in illegal possibility
I do not know what my greatest addiction can be
But the answer is now self evident to me
I'm addicted to life- what other choice can there be
I'm addicted to faith believing in what I do not see
I'm addicted to the comfort in what I choose to believe

The following 2 pieces are from email conversations shared with friends from an Internet Bipolar Chat/Support Group.

Eileen

I consider myself to be very lucky
My depression is my friend
He is always with me- even in my heights of mania
I know he is there- I accept he is there
And I know he will always be there to some degree
My morning star is my hope that I will make the best of life
no matter the time, the situation or distress
my morning star is my hope, my faith, my knowledge
knowledge of knowing that everything has it's cycle
the planets, stars and moons
my thoughts, my feelings and desires
all hinging on the light of hope
hope that things may be better
and if not
hoping that I at least made it a little better for myself-
or those around me
My depression is my friend, my acceptance of him brings hope
and this lights my way through even the darkest times
My morning star took many years to be seen by my naked eye
Born at the moment I was born
We all have a morning star
I only hope we all have the capability, or gain that ability, or find the tools to see it
eventually with time- the star grows with our hope, our faith, and our belief
that even in out darkest hour-
we have the capacity to shine

Michelle

Thank you !
Your appreciation is not needed but most welcome
And I hope you realize we all have a critical voice
created from echoes of others and our own regrets
I say- slap that bitch and tell it to shut up

You have gotten yourself to were you are today by your wits, knowledge and understanding
You are a survivor
you have over come many challenges and foes to get were you are today
each of us is a special gift to the world
unique in all our individual beauty
and you are no less entitled than any other soul upon this plane of existence
I pray we all work on our roads of acceptance
just by admitting our unique individuality
such a blessing life is-
but I swear
I have a few so called normal or uni-polar thinking friends
and they are the biggest group of BMW's I have ever seen
bitch moan and whine - but that is their lot

I believe we all have a greater capacity for understanding, love and acceptance due to our own challenges and survivorships

Yes- you are beautiful

Yes- you are worthy of being treated like a human being

Yes- you are a gift to each day- unique and blessed like the rose or lotus
which from the dung of life grows fragrant and beautiful blooms
each as unique as us

The Plight of Man

My Plight (my wild horses)

My life has always been a struggle
Even if it is with acceptance
Everyone, everyday is a survivor
if they face Dysfunction

Nothing wrong with being dysfunctional
I function just fine (so does everyone and everything)

Even if my depression never totally fades
Even if it grows to cloud my days

Even if my manic moments continue on
I continue to fight to accept myself all along

To say my depression has me so down I will cry
Whether it is chemical or due to life gone by

I will hate it
but accept it I must try
So that I can move on
and not be lost inside my mind.

There is no negative or positive unless I assign
A value or a feeling to that thought at the time

My mind will continue to be what it is
Like wild horses each free of bridal and bit
Each going wherever it's nature drives it

I cannot stop those horses upon the fly
I can only hope to choose on which one I will ride.

And if only to ride for a moment or two
Perhaps next time maybe minutes will do

Yet perhaps I may fall along the way
A hapless victim of natural display

Only to get up and try again today
Perhaps one day
I'll move beyond them anyway.

I Cannot Say……

I cannot say why my mind thinks this way
I cannot not say how logic and reason come into play
That they cannot carry the weight
I cannot speak the balance of this state
I cannot say how my reasoning works
It just works in a straight line dotted with curves
I cannot say what is the purpose to life
I cannot say my journey is left, wrong or right
I cannot say my road should be traveled by any other than I
I cannot say your suffering Is, or was, worse than mine
I cannot say that it was worse or better
I cannot grade life experiences with a simple letter
Or compare past to present without being bound by that tether
I cannot say today is the best no matter what came or follows
I cannot say life has been anything
other than breaths I have borrowed
I cannot say I won't try and make it better for myself
I cannot say I can make the best of what I have been dealt
I cannot say that is the purpose, the reason, for life in itself.

Spend

As I become more of the world
I am touched by its insanity
Echoing messages of desire,
Of lacking, of greed
I reach out to the one next to me
Only to find another consumer
One who uses without concern
Who seeks more than what he's earned
One like me as I've become
Seeking more than I have won
Never happy but for a moment
A new acquisition I have
But only this moment then I seek the new
Some not borrowed, stolen or true
The new become old
The comfort no longer hold
Driven to the new to be sold
People and things no difference unfold
New captures the desire over old
Lives lost, sold and bartered away
There is no value in humanity today
Except to spend, spend and spend away

Had I Only Known

Had I only known what life would bring
I would have packed a basket to watch the scene
Had I only known it was my choice
I would have spoke out loud in voice
Had I only known other would find fault
I too find fault with their assault
Had I only known that few accept their actions
I too would blame others for my infractions
Had I only known that I could choose to laugh
I would have chuckled over the tears that passed
Had I only known their problem wasn't mine
The bruises and injuries would have passed in no time
Had I only known that I can only react to thoughts in my head
I wouldn't have listened to what the voices said
Had I only known I could see life in any color
I would have a rainbow and no other
Had I only known that life required much work
I would have listened to the learned I had heard
Had I only known that man is perfectly imperfect
I would have accepted his design and purpose
Had I only known that I can choose to smile or frown
Nothing in this world could get me down
Had I only known that life was change
I'd pack a suitcase and be on my way
Had I only known that routines bring continuity
I'd break them all just to be free
Had I known I could set myself free
I'd cut the chains of mediocrity
Had I known back then what now seems to be
I would be someone different than whom I now see

A String of Pearls

Ceaseless minutes and eternal moments
Long lost days strung as pearls
Lost in the spaces tossed in the moment
Moments of ecstasy a string of pearls
Electric passions entwined in force
Unseen connections having no choice
Lost in the moment giving away the day
The freedom given away
No thought, no name
Only a pearl along the way
A sign left from the fray
A string of pearls across the mind lay

Tiny Bubbles

For Today and Tomorrow

Sometimes I just feel sick
Or better yet thick like a brick
Ashamed of what I have done
Ashamed of what I have missed
Following predictable patterns of self-sabotage
With guilt, sorrow and loss upon myself I heaped the blame
No other to choose what choices I have made
In the end it was I who chose my refrain
But the past cannot be lived in, as the present dies to the future
To try and accept who and what I am without disdain
To learn to love myself as can be done by no other man
Leave behind my losses, regrets sorrow and pain
They do no service to moving forward again
To live in a world so long gone by
Is to continually suffer and cry
Even if it was joyful times back then
It is a disservice to live continually in them
We have the capacity to live beyond habits, routines and echoes of the past
To grow beyond the pain that every life seems to have
And although our suffering seems so much worse than another possess
It's in learning to enjoy the journey that seems to be the test
Not a simple feat and insurmountable at best
So I'm feeling sick and thick as a brick
And I realize perhaps there might be a trick
To accept a past filled with emptiness, fear, pain, sorrow and regret,
Days and months even years self-torturing myself with many a bad habit
And the one thing that came to mind
If I did not judge myself I was fine
If I did not listen to those voices from a critical and learning past
That without those voices I was OK at last
I cannot say that this is an easy road
It is harder than diamonds but softer than gold
It is more precious and uplifting than can be extolled
To tell yourself you are OK and be your own best friend and advocate
Is the best present you could ever get
And no longer will you feel sick, thick as a brick, loss, regret or sorrow
But enjoy each day, and be whole again
for today and tomorrow

Equanimity

I would surrender
But not give in
I would share my world
And keep it for myself
To hold you in the moment
Releasing you to be free
To take what is given
To give without recompense
No design and no label
To be as it was meant
Nothing defined
Esoteric energies
Moments and eternities
I would surrender
You give into me
Loss gainfully
Caring caress be
Equanimity

Creatures of Habit

Creatures of habit
Trapped in the comfort of routine
Creatures of habit
Steps of repetition along life's path
Continuing oblivious to the ends wrath
Creatures of habit addicted to patterns
Of behaviors unrecognized or contemplated
For them it doesn't matter
That the mold can be shattered
Shattered to expose a new way
A new habit of habitual growth today
Creatures of habits we have all been at some time
So many and so few come to mind
Helpful or not helpful is my dividing line
And I fight my Creature of Habit time after time
Perhaps one day I will become the creature
as I see myself habitually becoming in my mind

Doing Nothing

Doing nothing
Just enough to get by
Changing when forced
Feeling powerless to try
A victim of circumstance
Everyone else the blame is cast
Wasted tomorrows like yesterday last
Lost in cyclic deprivation
The "doing nothing" equation
Instead of "something" you choose a way
To do as little as possible in every day
To surrender and concede is what is done
By doing nothing- nothing can be won
Choose to live in some agony
Or work to change what may be
To suffer in agony over the past
Or grow to accept you have survived it at last
To live exactly as your father did
Or move beyond your childhood
Do nothing and only the seasons change
Do something and accept change
Do nothing and it's only you to blame

Beyond the Past

I could blame my parents for many things
That I was abused or Mom ran to safety
But why would I choose to relive the injury
To traumatize myself continually
That does no service to anyone not even me
They could do no better with their options you see
Even though that changes nothing in the grand scheme
We were all children in some way
But I am an adult today, O.K.
Today I take the higher road
I release that burden I lighten my load
Freedom from the past just sold
Now the future is gold

Evolution

Evolution

First breath, step and word
Things not to be seen nor heard
Injury, Insult don't last
Step beyond the past
Accept the evolution into tomorrow
Learn the lessons from the tears, the joy and the sorrow
Let go of yesterday and grow for today and for tomorrow
Don't give into past regressions, obsessions, depressions
Because they are only echoes of impressions
Long lost and unchangeable shadows
Fight to live, live to love, love to grow
Accept, forgive and then you will know
Evolution evolves from what we know

Break the Mold

Break the mold and throw it to the floor
The vessel changes with each added drop
Changing design by each day's entry
Never the same again no mold is cast
Break the mild throw it to the floor
Same but different but not unique
Formed from the exterior the interior let be
Cast in an image created by some constrained design
Put upon the vessel expected to take the shape
Of subtle nuances of word and display
Shaped and cast by what came before
Trapped in a pattern repeated continually
The vessel was formed in cast of clay
Break the mold and throw it to the floor
To be a vessel created unique and distinct
Cherish the vessel made of clay
Be not formed from simple cast
Choose to be more than all the rest
Break the mold and throw it to the floor

Beloved Sister
(Kimberlye)

Dear sweet Sister I can see your smile
Not burned into a photograph but here all the while
Life was unfair and cruel to you
Not including what others had done too
You faced your challenges and life with grace
You championed the weak, the poor the hurt
You never complained nor said a word
You lived your life like a walking Christ
You gave of your time, effort, money and advice
I carry your memory and smile throughout every day and night
Oh so young for this life to end
SO I carry you with me till it comes my end
You have blessed and enriched my life and given more than I can pretend
You made my life better and that will never end
As I carry with me those memories long past
They remind me of you, your smile, your resolve and your laugh

Along the Road

The journey begins with one simple step
We fall and falter but yet no rest
Until we make unknown progress
We move ever faster in concentric circles
around an irregular universe
No faster, no slower, no better, no worse
We move forward time playing its verse
We choose the refrain in which we continually rehearse
But some move on to write in their own way
A brighter song to hear and display
Yet some are lost in the long past refrain
Held back by their own disdain
No better, no worse, just their way
Of walking the road of life today
Not accepting the path is always for one
Even when walking alongside who come
It is our path we must choose our steps
To fall and falter and steps retrace
Until we step beyond the stumbling place
Is just the natural state
The path is only as smooth as we make
The stones are steps or trips we choose
We make our best choice no win nor lose
Judgment hinders our shoes
To learn and grow makes them free and loose
It's is your path
So which do you choose
To run forward with hope and joy
To hold back like a lost girl or boy
To blame others for the steps you take
Or accept the lot you make
It's your path
Be a trailblazer
Leave a wake
Lighten your load
Dim not your way
By the darkness of yesterday
Instead light your path today
In a loving and forgiving way
And the path will be as smooth as glass
To mirror the light in which you have
The light you choose to color your path

Answers

All the answers I have found

I found within me

Resounding the response

What I found to be

It came on its own

It's unique voice I heard

From contemplations hard at work

Floating from the ether of thought

The answer came when I could see

The answer was always there within me

Waiting for the time to be shown
Obviously it remains unknown

Lost in folds of perception
Skewed in the minds deception

Forgotten in the days agenda
Millions of answers as many questions

Each a voice of unknown subjection
Who has the answers to the important questions

Would we listen or would we reject them

It's easier to find answers to order the world
Keeping it inside within ourselves

Never question the answers we have found
Considering ourselves on solid ground

To our answers we are bound

Addictions Wings

I know the excuses I have said them all
I've lived in my self-validation lies and all
Committed my existence beyond my control
Giving into the addiction and paying the toll
Losing moments and days lost and forgotten
Seeing as perfect instead the deathly begotten
Mind twisted around something so rotten
Days and years wasted and long gone
Into the vacuum of addiction I am drawn
Fighting to walk away from the scene
Weakness gives into the obscene
As all is lost in addictions regime
Hooked on the escape wanting to feel better
It starts so simply and ends rarely ever
Life and will no longer are mine
Seeking the high so I can hide
To fill the void I so often felt
Making me into something other than myself
Addiction demands will never end
Even being clean for a decade and then
I still hear the call of my addiction
I cannot deny it still carries a loud voice
But with work and understanding I have a choice
To fight my addiction and seek to be free
Face it head on and challenge it's voracity
See it for the villain I know it to be
I fill the void and move into today
Putting the present and past in their place
To move on for tomorrow and all I face
Without an addiction to fill the space
Which ransoms my future and present day
Because I wanted to feel better about yesterday
My addiction holds me back and rips me apart
But for today I will try and start
To live free no addictions a part
Of a life worthy of better things
Holding back addictions wings

The Path of Least Resistance

Be Divine

Children of Light are now being born
Into a world that seems destructive and worn
And soon will come the days of change
When the prophecies will come and remain
To build the world over and renew
Harmony before and after will ensue
It is unavoidable there is nothing to do
To stop the changes soon payable and due
So live in the positive light of the Divine
Know what comes was predestined sublime
Lost in prophesy of all faiths of God
Few see the signs others see it not
But it doesn't matter for all will see
That the goodness in each man will decree
His place beyond this age that be
This age will change Pieces will flee
The world will rock and the children of light will see
As action comes from the prophesies
And man will be weighed by his deeds
And it matters not the faith he believes
As the heart and mind is what is seen
By that view he will be judged accordingly
Have faith and do what is good Dear Divine Child
Hurt no man or leave them defiled
Give of your heart, your mind, money and time
Because the clock will not rewind
It moves forward to that predestined time
When all be judged even if no crime
Each to be weighed upon their merit and effort
By a being from beyond the earth
A being coming to call all it's children
Calling the faithful and the giving
Ending an era and creating a new beginning
The time is short so head these words
Be divine to everyone even if it hurts.
Nothing can buy what it is worth

I Cannot Change

I cannot change what I am,
I can only change how I react to this.
I cannot change how my mind works,
I can only change how I react to this.

I cannot change my past egregious behavior
I can only change how I accept myself.
I cannot change how my mind swings
But I can change and learn to accept these changes which are totally natural for me.

I cannot change any action I have done
But I can learn to love myself for the gift that I am.
I cannot accept guilt or feel guilty for actions in my past,
I can only admit I did the best I could with what I had.

I cannot any longer put myself down or hate myself because of this,
or any other challenge I have faced-
Because those experiences have created the person I am today- a survivor.
I cannot help others to find their way, until I myself understand the path I have followed.

I cannot do anything but love myself,
It is the worlds job to try and put me down, not mine.

I cannot accept anything but goodness from my friends,
I shall be a friend and so shall they.
I can no longer be my own worst enemy
How can I heal when I am conflicted?

I can only say I will try and love myself for all that I have done,
not done and everything in-between because no one- not even
me- has the right to judge what I don't understand or know.

I can only say "I like me, I like what I have been working towards, I like to tell anyone that if you cannot accept yourself- how do you expect others too.

I can only be my own best friend- because no one else knows me as well.
We tend to criticize ourselves for many reasons- but to what end?
Why not accept what we are and learn to recognize who
we truly are- then change is good and inevitable.

**If I could choose
(there is no other way)**

If I could choose to change or do it all over again
I would have to say NO to you my friend
Because this is the path that is meant for me
Without it I would not have learned to see how I now see
I would not have triumphed over the challenges there be
I would not have grown to me the man that is me
Instead to have taken the easier road
The road paved in comfort or so I am told
A path that is hidden and protected from the storm
A path that would leave me soft and unformed
Instead I choose to keep it all the same
Because without it I would not be where I am today
Each step bringing me along my way
And to seek to change the journey is to surrender, I say
I choose to move forward there is no other way.

The View

Apartment, Department, Compartmentalized,
Dirty, Clean, Sanitized,
Hanitized, Prized and Despised,
Whole, Part, Set-Aside,
Complete, Fractured, Dysfunctionalized,
Big picture now pixel size,
Obviously hidden in the light,
The view forgotten yet prized,
Only to be marginalized,
Hidden in view of the times,
Overlooked as attention declines,
Listening to words that cloud the eyes,
With smoke, mirror and lies,
No two see the same skies,
Situation, deviation or times,
His view is all he finds.

Because I Love You

Because I love you

you curse my days
you haunt my nights
you torture my soul
you are my light
It doesn't matter
where you've been
it only matters
I see you again
Every thought
comes back to you
I'm hopelessly helpless
Because I love you

Child of today

As a child I cried
But now I laugh with joy
Back then life was devoid
Now it is bright and alive
Once I hurt and held the pain
Finally it has been released for gain
Often it held me back to recall
Now I can learn and accept it all
I forgive because it helps to grow
I forgive and they have been told so
My inner child has finally been healed
Through effort and understanding I feel
That my childhood so full of abuse
Is the wellspring of blessings so true
Bringing strength to help me through
All the hardness that had ensued
I no longer am anchored to a past filled with pain
Looking back holding no disdain
To heal my child who now remains
Capable of living today better than yesterday
No longer do the injuries and insults have sway
Over my actions I carry with me today
What a blessed day Sweet Child of Today

The Muse

From the ether its shadow falls
Into the depths of inspiration it calls
Madness and creation it enthralls
Visions gain form from nothing at all.
No purpose other than to seek form
Something from nothing must be born
Driven out of the darkness from which it was torn.
Made unique and beautiful by artist hands
Driven by a force he cannot understand.
The toil of artist will not cease
Until the muse has finally been sent free
Leaving behind it's progeny
For all the world to see

It was You

Life was good back then
Memories warmer and lighter
Then world was my oyster
Great days always and akin
Till that spirit came in
Touched my soul created a smile
Looking at me all the while
Multi-colored layers and hue
It was you, it was you

Soft and gentle up turned tip
Passion and lust sailing ship
The viciously gentle kiss
Eternal moments this
It was you, It was you

The moment given freely
Connected beyond what can be
Connected thought, spirit, body and energy
No other moment can compare
Past memories can only despair
To the brilliance we did share
It was you, It was you

Now life is brighter still

Having shared to our fill
Not labeling what we feel
To grow and explore each day
Walk hand in hand part of the way
Smile, wink and nod our speech
Understanding what we speak
It was you, It was you

Tomorrow I will be alone
I was blessed to have known
Such a beautiful soul.
We have grown,
We have grown because
It was you, it was you
It was You

I cannot complain

I cannot complain about what I have
Memories, Injuries, Insults that last

I cannot compare what I do not know
My vision is skewed were my thoughts go

I cannot complain about what has happened to me
Everyone did their best including me

I dare not look back and seek to change
Because from then and now I am not the same

I won't relive past injury
Lost in trauma a vicious circle be

I won't complain over yesterday
I choose to move forward towards this day

I will not complain that life may seem hard
Because that is it's role it's only part

To challenge one to grow beyond the pain
To let go and to stop the complaint

But to live today with no judge in the ear
To tell myself what I need to hear

That life is a complaint if I choose it to be
Or I can make it better by setting myself free

To work hard to live positively
Seeking the knowledge that is unseen

That if I complain I give away my power indeed
And lose my life again to thee

Then I will complain to be set free.

The Shape Shifter

Agreeable yet contrary
Friend sometime adversary
Willing yet stubborn
Ignorant sometimes to learn

Rich and poor in a myriad of ways
Driven and focused still to laze
Answer with contradiction
Fact yet fiction

Possessed with unseen truth
Believing only what it can use
Self centered and giving
One but fractured living

No single thought to remain
Even though a familiar refrain
Solid yet a quivering mass
Moving forward through the past
Lost in a moment eternity to last

The shape shifter moves in liquid cement
Anchored by the foot in the moment
Always the same but in constant change
Solid logic lost in mental derange

Not knowing what he display
Thinking himself a molded array
The shape shifter exterior so stiff
Inside the jelly rests and sits

The name of the one who shape shifts

Man, Yes Man, it is

Fractured

True Love

To give freely without recompense
To support without defense
To share freely in the moment
No guilt, shame or embarrassment
Without tether or form of chain
Singing it's ecstatic refrain
Better to share the moment that be
For moments fall into eternity
And are also fleeting you see
Enjoy the love for what it be
Intrinsic value of sentimentality
That comes so few and far between
Precious and fleeting few have seen
True love given without any strings
No demands but to give and receive
Coming from within the souls energy
True love sacrifices itself freely
Knowing that in the giving does it receive
The joy true love brings.

Deja Vu

I've been here before
it must have been a dream
it feels so familiar
liked I've lived this scene

Out of nowhere
it hit me blind
I've been here before
but only in my mind

Shocking and familiar
Nightmare out of time
a second visitation
but only in my mind

this time it's real
not just a movie scene
I know I've been here before
or am I living a dream

The Ship

Upon a sea of glass
The tide gives way
Then gives back
As the winds break the void
Waters rise without choice
The ship buffeted
There is no recourse
Stand fast echoes the voice
Winds yell and scream
The ship rises to fall into obscurity
To be lifted again
To see the horizon
Lost as quickly as won
And the winds of life howl against the little ship
Horizon or not the ship must continue on
No matter what elements obscure the course
The ship gives not into the relinquishing force
Even if temporarily abated
Sail on till the sails no longer billow
The engine no longer bellow
The body has become tattered and torn
Ancient aching and worn timbers be
But what a journey
Thanks for staying true to your course
This aching body decree.

Love's Toll

I will love
who you are
how you are
why you are
what you are
my love has no stop
it has no start
it just is
like we are
comfortable together
through all weather
I'll stand beside you dear
If necessary I will stand clear
to give you room to breathe and grow
and share in all that we know
I give my heart, mind, body and soul
Because I can love till death takes it's toll

Your Memory Torments Me

V1
It made me smile
to hear your voice
It made me cry
you made your choice
Chorus
Your memory torments me
kills me to the bone
I can't go on with you
I can't just let you go
V2
I carry on
alone again
I see your smile
In my head
V3
Miles and days away
you still torment me
anytime of day
If only you stayed

Where lies your power?

Energy of thought feeding desire
Giving away or keeping the fire
Where lies the power?
Accepting or assigning blame
You keep or give away the flame
Whatever comforts, whatever keeps you sane
Possessing or giving away
Where lies your power today?
Powerless or powerful it's your day
Proactive or reactive you choose the way
To forgive or to hate is your say
Where lies your power today?
To go forward or backward you control
To laze in ignorance or knowledge your goal
Lost in a past experience or projected future role
Where does your power live – today, yesterday or tomorrow?
Now I am empowered to forgive the past
Giving myself and others their power back
Those days sway no more power over me
And that's the way it should be.
My power lies anchored to tomorrow

It's a New Day

V1
I was a jerk
I was a fool
I can't forget
What I do
Chorus
It's a new day
Maybe it's changed
It's just so strange
What can I say
V2
It's been bad
Its been worse
It could be better
But it hurts
V3
If I knew then
what I know now
changing nothing
I don't know how

Those Echoes of Childhood

Echoes from days past ring in my ear
Feeding guilt and shame as their echo resounds
Words of condemnation, teaching and love
Pain and suffering as I give into their sway
Judge and executioner taking their space
The rings resound the words unclear
The action my mind had to take
Giving into the oration each having its way
To hear the reverberations of childhood's day
Better to grow old and let it all fade
Those echoes of childhood must be let go
As childhood into adulthood grows
Their purpose is no longer needed
I will not use them to feel defeated
Or left alone, abused and cheated
Instead I let it all go today
To forgive what I cannot say

Society

Maybe it's just me

V1
I saw you there
that cold cruel day
You like sunshine
pierced the gray

Chorus
Are you real
or just a fantasy
could it be you
maybe it's just me

V2
That smile those eyes
Pierced me deep inside
I couldn't believe my eyes
you a figment of my mind

V3
you curse my dreams
torment my days
I feel you next to me
so real you seem

V4
nothing is perfect
not in any reality
you make me better
my aspiration my dream

V5
one day I'll find you
brighter than the sun
and I will rest easy
my torment done

Open the Windows

clean the attic
clear the deadwood
make way for tomorrow
yesterday done and good

Chorus
Open the windows
clear some space
let in the light
look at the new face

V2
put away yesterday
live in today
hoping for tomorrow's
trouble along the way

V3
put away today
work for tomorrow
learn from the past
let go the sorrow

V4
let in the air and light
change your routine or sight
make way for tomorrow tonight
live in the time of your chosen delight

Perfectly Imperfect

I knew I grew
then it stopped
ruler of my destiny
whatever I want

Chorus
Perfectly Imperfectly
We really are
standing so tall
falling so far

V2
I felt the victim
I believed it true
victimizing myself
the things I do

V3
Can't stop the waves
Can learn to surf
sometimes I survive
sometimes it's worse

Primordial Waters

Scatter the Ashes

Chorus
Scatter the ashes
to the 4 winds
what has been
never again

V1
yesterdays memories
a lifetime away
yesterdays sorrows
no longer pay

V2
today's dream
is tomorrows truth
today's memories
get me through

V3
tomorrows world
created from yesterday
a heartbeat away
from today

V4
Scatter the ashes
remains on the wing
always beginning
the death of a dream

Razors Edge

Living on the Razor Edge
Torn between hurt and pain
Lost in the moment
living what has been
Walking between love and joy
Keep balance my boy
living between the night and day
head in the future your feet stay
in this moment called today
lost today from yesterday
choose direction I say
today, tomorrow or yesterday
Walking the Razors Edge
Path to where I am going
footsteps of where I have been
On the edge till the end
Exactly where I began
Every choice a new line of sight
Walking the edge left to right
Following even depth and height
The edge, the path, is only mine
A tight rope through time
giving my life outline
The edge is the crux of my mind
in deciding where I turn this time
But it only cuts if I choose
Or walk upon it without shoes
Always as narrow or wide as I believe
Capable of nothing or making me bleed
The edge is whatever I believe
That cuts through life for me
Creating a way for me to breathe
and trim away the crap of life
or cut myself down if I like
Expressed in what I do
capable of damaging others too
Anything might help or harm
It's my edge, my choice, my arm!

The Darkness

V1
Dark days and darker nights
Seeing things in the blindness
That is hidden in the light
Dark days and darker nights

Chorus
In the darkness
Even the light hurts
Everything costs something
For whatever it's worth

V2
The dawn comes
but no light to be seen
Even in the daylight
I can see my dreams

V3
Darkness end soon
Bring back the light
The Darkness I fight
Aching for the light

V4
Darkness ends
The light kills
Deep nto my soul
Darkness rolls

The Pace Quickening

The pace quickening

The race already begun

It's not over never to be won

The whirlwind takes some

Leaving others in dust

It comes from nowhere

None knows where it ends up

Be prepared and ready for the storm

It will come so fast no time to warn

The warning came long ago

Be prepared for you never know

When the winds of time will blow

Taking you to where you do not know

Fulfilling the destiny of your soul

Desert(ed) River

Till I no longer breathe

I want to know your depth of your love
The heights of your spirit from above
The width of your knowledge of life
The lengths you have survived

I want to see your smile everyday
To hear every word you have to say
To taste your kisses in every way
To feel your breath upon my face

I want to know how you feel
To think with confidence love is real
To want to grow old with you
To desire all that you do

I want to see your beautiful face
To show you none could take your place
To give back the smile you give to me
To live this till I no longer breathe

No comfort in comfort
(Kimberlye)

Today marks a year my sister spent in comfort
Not limited by a world to surround her
Not torn by the winds of life that blow
Never to live again, to struggle and grow

Still in memory she is divine
She struggles no more in spirit, body and mind
Eventually the comfort will come to me in time
But I live not in comfort or luxury to find

I grow onward facing the march of time
Not lost in comfort but to struggle to survive
To grow beyond routines that time define
To reach beyond the patterns within my mind
And reach out to comfort though it is not yet my time

I cannot spend my days in ease
Lost in patterns and personal routine
I seek to grow beyond what I now me
To push forward in knowledge I need to succeed
Because life holds no moment of comfort you see
I cannot sit back waiting for comfort to find me

I will live each moment beyond past possibility
I will not find comfort till comfort finds me
I cannot rest or give in to complacency
I must grow, live and learn as much as there be
Till the moment that comfort finally touches me

I shall make a mark in life like a line on the beach
And when I reach it again I shall have finally achieved
Comfort that is well deserved you see

I cannot rest until that comfort touches me

Stagnant Rain Drops

Stagnant rain drops fill my soul
Tears of sorrow down my cheek did roll
As I smelled the musky waters fill my mind
Dirty emotions I though I had left behind
Stagnant raindrops that water my world

Can beauty from pollution grow
I say how can it not be so
Drop the rain drops as stagnant as they be

Water, feed and nurture me
Stagnant raindrops condensed from my eternal see
Falling again from a past I thought I was free
And so I smell the dark dank waters as my spirit is drenched
And flowers grow where the spirit is now quenched
Making things new, beautiful, and to grow again
From the stagnant waters of my past do they fall

But today, although it quenches, it is not necessary at all
To wade through flooding waters that rain down
That no longer suffocates me, not this time around

Beauty grows in ugliness abound
It knows not what nourishes the ground
But grows beyond those stagnant drops that fall
To show me beauty can always be found
Even in stagnant waters all around

We too can grow beyond the stagnant waters of the past
And flourish in adversity as the lotus has
Living in dung or trash along the way
Not hindered by where it's roots stay
Or the force of growth necessary today
Or from where the waters come from to bring life it's way
Stagnant waters nourish as they fall away

From the Heights

My Hope

My Hope is that thought that gives me the desire to carry on

My Hope is knowing that faithfully things will come into balance

My hope is that even though I cannot feel today- I will feel someday

My Hope is knowing that even though I cannot go back
I look to the future
My Hope gives that future possibility

My Hope is that today may be better or worse than yesterday,
but not the same tomorrow

My Hope is that I will accept I am where I am supposed to be

My Hope is always wanting more than what I already have

My Hope is that I accept the day for what it is
My Hope is that I learn to accept where I am today

My Hope is that I will learn something about myself and others
My Hope is that my observations bring me wisdom, comfort, laughter

My Hope is that my Higher Power will see my need
My Hope is that the universe will provide
My Hope is that I find peace in the moment
My Hope is that I will love myself as I am

My Hope is that I have been given intellect that I will know how to use
My Hope is that when my struggle finally ends- it is not my end
My Hope is all who suffer find relief

My Hope is all who pray find their God and their answers

My Hope is that even at my worst extreme I will not lose sight of the center
My Hope is that I learn to listen to those who care

My Hope is that I learn to love myself in this moment
My Hope is that that love will never end
Till Jesus comes back again.

Hope Falls

Web Articles and Presentations published at DropDeadHappy.com

What's the price of your self-esteem?

It seems that most of my friends echo a theme that I have often heard repeated in so many ways in social settings and in numerous support and help groups.

What echoes in my ear is that everyone seems to feel shame on some level. Why is this? Certainly shame devalues us and our self esteem. Certainly regret is a 1/2 step before shame but why do people invest the effort to complete this trip? As adults we should learn to accept and love who we are and what we have done! Otherwise we only hold ourselves back from change and/or progress in this life. So often the cause of this shame is based in our childhood and is often the echoes of voices that taught us from right and wrong. Well unless you came from my family that should be true, my family, a nuclear family that blew apart long before I was 7. So I guess I was blessed never to have that supervision and to only known shame through the taunts of classmates. But there is no shame for me because my investment in my self worth is to use my energy to develop self-pride and self-respect. Certainly this sounds like a difficult task- and it is- even for one who admits no shame. For one, me, who invested the price of time and effort to support my belief that shame has no place in life, yes regret may have, but shame devalues every bit of self esteem and takes away from the beautiful and unique being I am.

I remember a time when my Grandmother was teaching me to read and write, to fight the ADD and Dyslexia, and having been forced by my father to use my right hand because as he said many times "No son of mine is going to be a lefty freak". I asked her "Grandma, am I a freak?" She responded with the wisest words I have ever heard- "No you are perfect, perfectly imperfect. Just the way God made you!" and with that one statement she invested in my self-esteem and it has paid off everyday of my life. Yes we are all perfectly imperfect. Forget the shame, learn and grow through your regrets and invest in your own self esteem. Pride creates self worth and shame devalues it!

What do you invest in your self-worth? Your self-esteem?

Because this is wealth or debt you place upon yourself.

The problem isn't stress!!! - (No Joke - even if funny)

Go ahead and call me a fool but I can prove this statement "the problem isn't stress!"

You may question my sanity but the plain fact is that stress is a fact of life and if you deny that then we have to deal with a new problem (called denial).

So, I am no fool to recognize and accept this fact. And the truth being said, "the real problem is that we need quick, simple, inexpensive, and especially effective, ways to counter the stress response. This response occurs from all types of physical, mental and emotional forces in or lives and we often live in this state for much longer than we should eventually manifesting itself in our own discomfort, loss of energy, time and sometimes affects our health, wealth and living.

How do I know if I am living in this stress response? Tell me - do you feel like you are on vacation or do you notice quick thoughts, heartbeat or breathing?

Our modern lives have evolved faster than our inherent human traits so we respond to modern stress as the caveman responded to stress in his body- the racing heart, breath and thoughts as the body goes to alert and remains there. But our ancestors also had time to rest and break the cycle of racing thoughts, breathing and heartbeat. We modern people often feel we have to little time and monies to do something for our well-being as we prioritize other things ahead of ourselves.

I know that exercise may be one of the best ways of all to help deal with the stress of modern life even if it may reintroduce our bodies to other types of stressors.

But inducing the an thesis, the killer, of this stress response takes little time and little effort because all we are doing is learning a mental trick to relax the mind which in turn relaxes the body which in turn reduces our physical and mental stress response giving us back our power of relaxed control and focus.

For many years I worked overseeing Clinical trials of new medications in patients having to record any noteworthy events that occurred to any of our study participants.

This was a very stressful job as it was a very small office and my employment required I do everything except for what was required by the doctor (Primary Investigator) You talk about stress, after 3 months my hair committed suicide. But then I started utilizing these simple techniques that helped me create a more relaxed and efficient environment at work and at home even while my partner was dying of AIDS.

There are many labels for visualization and many forms of meditation but to me they are one in the same and serve the same purpose. The most common misconception of mediation is that one is trying to clear the mind of thought and this is so untrue because our minds do not stop.

The trick is to try not to "attach" to the thought but if you do it is OK just return back to your focus without guilt, blame or judgment. Experienced mediators, like Buddhist Master and Teacher Geshe Kelsang Gyatso, admits that even after years, a lifetime, of meditation he still experiences at least 17 thoughts during a 20-minute meditation.

But we do not need that long at all the slow and even stop our stress response simply by following a simple routine and all you need is a minimum of 30 seconds.

All meditation has a focus or something that we visualize within our minds. Sadly we cannot do this in a car but maybe you could, at home or office, visualize yourself being at peace while stick in rush hour traffic. The focus can be anything from having stronger personal traits, interpersonal skills, a garden or my favorite- the eternal vacation. Because in my employment I didn't take vacations until forced because of the demands and responsibilities it required. I would visit another vacation spot each time I utilized a little mediation break. After 5 years I had traveled 3 times around the world and it lasted 6 years in total.

Even 30 seconds on the beaches of the Cancun, Hawaii, Australia and everywhere in between from the forest of Costa Rica to the penguins of the South Pole. And man it was the best vacation I ever had and I was able to manage many clinical trials with up to 400 patient visits every month.

So now remember that thoughts will happen and try not to attach to them and if you do it is OK because there is no judgment when we do this because we are humans with incredible minds. I also had my secret garden (with my secret friends) and also gained strength in traits I felt weak in.

Here are the steps I follow:
1. pick my focus object, place or desire
2. sit or lie in a comfortable position hands resting in my lap or in each other
3. close my eyes,
4. take a deep breath in and focus on the point where the air enters my body (a momentary focus point to make us aware of or body while slowly breathing in and out) I take 3 breaths focusing on the sensation of the air as it rushes pat the tip of my nose (or lips if nose is stuffed up)
5. go to my focus I had set in the beginning
6. do this for a minimum of 30 seconds
7. return to the breathing and the point where it enters your body for another 1-3 breaths.

It can be difficult to stop the thoughts but in the very beginning I visualized a large aquarium with every color of fish and that as thoughts arose they were just another colorful fish going by. And often I get lost in that thought and just return to my focus. This not only helped me deal with stress but also helped me identify errant, destructive and non-productive thoughts my bipolar mind would throw at me and give me a little modicum of control over the most debilitating ones.

So I believe I have proved that stress isn't the problem, exercise although very beneficial isn't required and we can all gain some modicum of control, relaxation and empowerment in our lives and employment.

Who is to blame?

One statement that always makes me laugh is when I hear someone say "You made me do it" or "You made me mad".

Do you see anything comically wrong with these statements? Certainly when uttered as children those statements seem apropos.

But I outgrew childhood in my childhood and realized that these statements simply state "I am powerless to control myself" (so I will blame you).

And truly when we blame others for our actions we give away our power and gain nothing and can learn nothing of ourselves from the experience. I recently was at a friend's house and he asked if I had made him mad by the jokes he was hoisting at me about my baldness. I replied "No, I do not give you that power over me" and continued "in fact the only thing I am mad about, but have long since accepted, was that I hated losing my hair. In fact my friend" I continued "it was hard in high school because everyone thought I was a nark. My anger was not at him but at my genetics and how hard it made it for me to try and fit in during high school.

Simply admitting where my emotions had come from I had learned something about myself and kept my own power over the situation and we had a wonderful evening and come to a deeper understanding of each other. Often time's people assign blame to others simply so they do not have to face their own personal truths being blinded by the lies they tell themselves instead of facing the true reality.

I choose to live in reality and not as a Queen of Denial and all that I do and have done and will do cannot be blamed on anyone either than myself. And none other can be commended or praised for actions. Instead of blaming others I prefer to look at what I did and try to understand why.

SO that no matter what happened, even if I did get mad and caused some type of damage, I learn from it and work towards change and understanding. If I cannot understand myself how can I truly understand others?

In my Pozitive Speaking presentation which I have shared with hundreds, or more, I admit I was infected even before we had the name of H.I.V. and when asked who Infected me I reply "I did, because even in those days when we didn't know much about this dis-ease I was the one playing with my life my injecting drugs. I knew of other risks but no matter the knowledge at that time- I did this to myself".

Even in this day and age you cannot tell if someone is infected so I beg you to always take personal responsibility. I can blame no one else but myself.

Possibilities

I'm Bored !!!

I hear this from time to time from the few friends I have left who have survived living with HIV/AIDS. I have survived taking meds since 1986. And, yes, at times, I have said the same thing myself - I am BORED. When in fact, in my mind, I was simply lazy.

It seemed easier to be a BMW (B!#CH, Moan and Whine) than to do something, anything, to take away my boredom. And certainly living in a rural area, as I do now, where my nearest neighbor is ¼ mile away and the community consist of a meeting hall, 3 churches, post office and a small convenience store.

But I have never been bored here even though I consider myself lazy. Because boredom comes from stagnancy, from not doing or growing on some level or by being stuck in the same routine without taking a break. And perhaps it is my desire to continue to grow that I rarely ever feel bo red.

When I am bored I ask myself:
1. what can I do that is different than yesterday
2. what can I learn that interest me
3. what can I express in some way

I find myself sitting outside in the evening watching the beauty as the sun goes down and reflecting on the accomplishments of the day. Every days accomplishments are always a little different if you really analyze it logically.
I turn of the T.V. or radio and just enjoy the silent moment before I start reading a topic of interest. And since you are reading this I can only presume you have access to the worlds largest library- the internet.
 And sometimes I will just pick up the flute and try and trudge my way through a song.

Boredom comes from apathy and not only screams for actions but also can kill the desire to act. SO if your bored try something new, experience something old, or simply sit back, be lazy and wallow in your misery driving your BMW right through your natural desire to continue to grow on some level.

Having lived in the city as well as rural area I know that boredom is baggage that is always waiting to be taken out. Instead take out your curiosity, your wonder, your desire, your interest, your hopes and dreams and explore those pieces of baggage instead. It might just be a pleasant surprise.

Who is driving the bus?
(and why is it smoking???)
(a story of addiction and attraction)

I am biting my nails trying not to follow the urge to get some cigarettes. I have a little money and I have enough gas to make it but I don't want to identify with being a smoker.

I don't care if there is some weight gain because that is only permanent if I choose. So every time that urge comes I tell myself to focus on something else so as to divert my attention to the current thought of wanting to have a cig. I don't want to attach to that urge anymore, not show the physical signs and its affect on me.

It's tough learning to detach from a thought especially if it has become a pattern of always reacting to the same situation in the same way. It's like I set a bus route in my mind, into a computer, and whenever I meet a certain obstacle I deviate from my original path in a preprogrammed way.

I want to be the driver of my bus as much as possible, I don't want to sit back and relax or be a back seat driver. I want to have the control to choose which direction I will take my bus load that comprises the many facets of who/what I am. Because if I can do in reality what I hope to do in my mind I must make a concerted effort to do more driving and not let the preprogram take control in its customary ways.
Sure I cannot stop the preprogramming but make the effort to keep in control.
I know I will never totally succeed as the programming is always there, always on and always alert.

I can only hope to work to navigate with it and choose how I will attach my actions once the programming does kick in. And I've basically been addicted to nicotine since puberty- 35 years- so the programming is strong.

But I have done it before, I know it is possible as I have used it to deal with major bouts of panic and anxiety that at one time hindered me employment.

BTW that job required driving so I guess that's why I use the bus analogy- besides I like considering myself so multifaceted that I require a bus for each facet.

Don't Forget to Breathe
(a speech performed for the Toast Masters Word Warrior Group and also published at DropDeadHappy.com)

Why is it when ever you are most stressed some genius comes up and says "Don't forget to breathe?"

I could see them saying that if I were lying on the floor. But perhaps there is wisdom in this moronic saying, "Don't forget to Breathe". Maybe what they are telling you in a bass awkward way is "Hey- take a deep breath".

It seems we rarely consider our breathing since it happens whether we think about it or not. But every athlete, musician and speaker knows that the foundation for their successful achievement starts with proper breathing.
Now I am sure you rarely ever think of your breathing but your state of breathing can be an indicator of stress.
Deep breathing is the foundation of most self-relaxation, meditation and biofeedback techniques.

Tonight I share a stress reduction technique which only requires as little as 15 seconds. And then we will add a few twist to increase the relaxation effect.
But I promise this technique won't put you to sleep but instead will allow you return to your tasks at hand in a more alert yet relaxed state.
And you can do this technique anywhere although I wouldn't suggest trying it while driving on route 62 or Old Woman Springs Road.

The fact is we live in 2 states of being and these are the relaxed state- as if you were on vacation and the stressed state which is anything other than being relaxed.
We shall also do an exercise which can pinpoint where stress may be affect you without your even being aware of it.
With deep breathing our bodies not only attain more oxygen per breath and release more Carbon Dioxide and other toxins but also promotes alertness and concentration skills.

Now lets see how you breathe. I would like you to sit up straight as if there is an invisible wire hanging from the ceiling which goes through the top of your skull and runs all the way down your spine. Now put one hand on your chest and one below the rib cage.

That's great because you are already ½ there.

DON'T FORGET TO BREATHE (continued)

For those of you who felt your chest or shoulders rise need to try it again. This time lets all imagine that the breath we take in is filling a balloon which is being filled by our bog toes. Now lets all take a long slow breath in and see if we notice any changes.

Some of you may notice- Wow I've never seen my stomach that big. Others may be having difficulty but with practice you can learn to take deeper and slower breaths as 1 step in your stress management.

In the process of being a student of Buddhist meditation we learn that everything starts with the breath. Now the purpose of mediation isn't to clear your mind but to focus the mind. And expect extemporaneous thought to come up in your mind during this exercise because we cannot control what the mind may think only what we do about it.

And we cannot control our stress but we can learn to manage it more effectively.
Now lets take a little stress break and I hope you will follow my guidance.

Sit up straight, not strained but comfortable. Rest your hands in your lap and close your eyes.
Now focus on the tip of your nose and feel as you breathe in slowly and deeply.

Hold it for a second and slowly let it out. If you cannot breathe through your nose right now then focus on your top lip as the air move in and out. It is truly better to use the nose as the physiologic response is different than breathing through the mouth.

Now we are taking our 3rd deep breath and we can focus on something else.
Now don't forget to breathe and keep breathing slowly.
Now lets just imagine that perfect vacation. Where would you want to start. Keep breathing and focus on that vacation that you might never take. Experience what you feel it would be like, the smells, taste.

Ok now the vacation is over and time to take another deep breath and think to yourself- I am calm, I am relaxed and I am in control.
For years I took a vacation often many times a day and after 4 years working in a very demanding health care job I had a 17 year vacation.

DON'T FORGET TO BREATHE (continued)

And now to show you were your hidden stress lies is very simple. We start the same way by breathing and focusing on where the breath enters and leaves our bodies. Now we tense and relax areas of our bodies but one small area at a time beginning with the forehead tighten then relax, the jaw, the neck, shoulders, arms, hands, fingers, chest, buttocks, thighs calves and feet. Slowly work your way down and if anything feel tense then that's were some of your stress is hidden. As you relax each muscle it's good to think "I relax this muscle and release it's stress.

So from a simple breathe be not only live and exist but can accomplish great things. And one thing we should all strive to accomplish is utilizing some form of stress management. I hope that you don't forget to breathe, enjoy taking deep breaths and start experiencing that vacation you may never actually take.

Foot Steps

The Aggravation of Expectation

I always have expectations and for the most part they have served me well.

Well, that is provided I only weight them upon myself. It seems my greatest disappointments have come from my greatest expectations. And it always seems that they weren't expectations I placed upon myself but upon others. Still it seems there is a double standard here, and perhaps it is expected, that I have different expectations for myself and for everyone else. And even within those 2 categories there are varying degrees of expectation in every situation.

Years ago I suffered debilitating Anxiety and as soon as I felt that first twinge of panic I could do nothing but expect the Anxiety to rule. But one day I realized that part of my condition was my expectation of it's continuation requiring medication to relieve the duress. I wanted things to change, I expected them to change, but I knew that change can only come from within. I expected that I could find a way to deal with these events so that I could remain in control. I expected that I had greater control that what I did until I realized that that expectation only limited my success. I had to see and expect myself to be able to recognize the onset of panic and think differently. To no longer see and expect myself to be out of control because I would no longer be out of control when that happens. I know exactly how it feels when it starts and I breath and remind myself that nothing is so serious, no thought so provoking, that my body and mind should be thrown into a tempest.

I expected it to happen and I expected that control could also happen.

Perhaps its isn't simply that we have expectation but that we choose what we will expect.

When I expect my friends to be exactly who they are I get the luxury of seeing them in their natural state. When I expect them to fit into some preconceived role then I am expecting them to be actors. If I expect them to treat me as I would them then I am not giving them the chance to be human, to error, make mistakes and expect them to understand the understandable.

I battle with expectations everyday dealing with HIV, Bipolar Affective Disorder and, for the last 5 months, chronic pancreatitis. Friends and family ask me "How can you always be of such good spirits and feeling that life is blessed' and I say "I expect that life is blessed…and it is"

The Winds of Change

The Winds of Change envelop me
Drive me to places and times I cannot tell
Force me into unseen times as well
The Winds of Change buffet me
Pushing me onward
Onward through Eternity
The Winds of Change become Me
As I relent to their ferocity
The Winds of Change move me
I have no choice floating on Life's Sea
Than to hope to navigate the unseen
The Winds of Change that be

The Banquet

Even though I am Bipolar with HIV/AIDS I realized recently I am more like my friends than I had hoped. And this has nothing to do with anything aesthetic instead it has to do with the way we treat ourselves and perceive what must be done.

A dear friend has 3 art shows coming up and she stresses herself out thinking about everything that has to be done. She often says "I have got to start this and that and the other. Oh there is so much to do and so little time!!! I have got so much on my plate but I don't know where to begin!"

"With one bite at a time" was my response and she laughed. "You know you're right DeWayne- if I just take it one bite at a time I'll get through it". I think sometimes we put extra weight upon ourselves perceiving our "plate" to be filled with more than we can chew. But if we take it a little at a time- even just a little everyday- we will accomplish clearing that plate or task.

It is your choice to see your plate ½ full or ½ empty or simply loaded or as light as a feather or heavier than death. It doesn't matter who you are, or what challenges and/or Dysfunctions you face. It only matters how you choose to see what is on your plate.

Life is a banquet and you choose the menu!
(I just love all the tastes, smells and colors of Dysfunction so yummy, unique and filling.)

Hard Water

In That Light

If I carry the weight of yesterday
How can I be free today
If I anchor myself to the past
How far can I sail forward at tack
If I live in days gone by
How many pass without try
If I place myself in shame
How can I defend my name
If I see myself with no fault
How can I tell the truth at all
If I give freely to you
How can I expect return anew
If I choose to believe in you
How can I keep expectations few
If I choose to see black or white
How can I not see it in that light
If I can change my perspective and view
How can I not marvel at me and you

Keep The Bridges

Don't burn the bridges
as you make new roads
remember where you came
you might have to go back again

Just let things go along the way
walk your path with faith I say
Don't be pitiless counting pennies
count the uncountable myriad of things

life is more than what's been
filled with surprise unexpected
the only thing that gets hurt
is our expectation at worst

Keep the bridges
don't burn them down
they serve a purpose
even if none can be found

The Smile

V1
You keep wandering across my mind
It can happen at any time
With hope and joy I see your smile
Wanting more all the while

chorus
But it's not my choice
It's up to you
To see the love looking through
The eyes that keep smiling at you

V2
I don't know what to say or do
Because I don't know the real you
I want to give in and digress
But I won't break my heart again

V3
I take the chance and open the door
Telling you that I want so much more
I have to try I cannot wait
In love there is no time to waste

V4
You look back with that smile
And came to me in loving style
Now that smile never leaves
In mind and body you with me

V5
I cannot express the depth
Of our joy and happiness
2 for 1 is our bliss
Smiles never end

Fighting the Power (of Expectation)

Honestly I have enough trouble keeping up with the expectations I put upon myself! And I even know what those expectations are, even though, I don't expect, I will share them today!

I write about Expectation a lot because I believe it is often the biggest harm producer not only to our personal identity but also our interaction with others. But the problem isn't that we have these Expectations since it is the natural state of our minds to create them. Most of these are created when our mind recognizes a pattern and then can Expect an outcome.

Expectations are a hope of an outcome. but I believe we often put to much weight, or blame, into an outcome that doesn't meet our Expectation. If it's cloudy you Expect rain and it does not come you cannot assign blame to the cloud. You can only assign blame to your expectation.

Don't let your Expectations cause undue blame in your relationships or stop you from getting to know the real person behind the clothes. Just because most of my clothes may have holes don't Expect me to be anything other than a human like yourself......it's tough being HumanKind but it helps to start with yourself.

The Silence Song

V1
Can you stand the sound of silence
Does it ring in your ears
Does it possess your waking moment
Or is it only in your tears

Chorus
The sound of silence screams out loud
A voice screaming above the crowd
The sound of silence falls on deaf ears
No one misses what they cannot hear

V2
Is there always noise and chaos
Do you ever take a moment off
Tell me what rings in your ears
Because silence is all that I hear

V3
I want to hear the rumble and noise
The incessant tumult that often annoys
Or the hum of the lights as I go by
Anything but silence for just one night

V4
I'd give up the void of calm and peace
If someone were worth such a feast
Sharing the quiet and noisy riot
Breaking the silence between us

Survival of the Fittest

Scatter The Ashes

V1
Little child's eyes
Wonder to subside
Poor little child
Childhood dies

Chorus
Scatter the ashes
Crash and burn
There's just today
Tomorrow will turn

V2
Evil to Legal
Leave your mark
Time is passing
End to start

V3
Days the same
Years of routine
Predictable me
Holding nothing

V4
Just a heartbeat
It could all end
Or just change
Alone again

V5
Waste and ashes
From everything
Nothing left
Only me

The Fly

V1
Your life an eternity
But lost in a moment
Free to Fly today
Till you met your torment
With a quick or slow end

Chorus
Free to Fly
Fly on the wind
Oh little fly
Where have you been

V2
Living off crap
What can I say
Fly on the wind
Wherever you may
All you have is today

V3
Learn or Die
Before it ends
Oh little fly
you are like me
my dear little friend

V4
Oh little fly
I fly like you
But I have no wings
To carry me through
Still I am just like you

V5
From delight to delight
Fly the Fly and I
Living off what we find
Doing the best in time
Until the moment we die

This article was published 12/1/2006. This article was the headliner of section B, local section, of the Desert Sun.
The preeminent and only newspaper for Palm Springs and the Coachella Valley.
After many attempts I discovered that scanning the article looked great on my PC but when went in email only the picture ass legible.
So I cut the picture and typed the article verbatim.

Facing the AIDS virus head on. By Stephanie Frith

Sometimes he wonders if it would have been better if he had died 10 years ago.

If he had he wouldn't wake up every morning wishing to talk to friends who are no longer around.

Friends who have died from complications relating to the AIDS virus. The same virus DeWayne Benson has had for over 20 years. The same virus that forces him to take as many as 15 pills per day. The virus that has affected his liver, his pancreas, his social life. His ability to work.

"People think it's easy to survive this long, but it's a sad and lonely life" said Benson, who sat for an interview recently at The Desert AIDS project, where he is a client and volunteer. Today is World AIDS Day. Benson isn't a spokesman for the international day of commemoration for more than 25 million who have died from AIDS and 40 million people living with HIV/AIDS worldwide.

But, the Palm Springs man, in flannel shirt, jeans, tennis shoes and wire-rimmed glasses knows what more than 7,400 people living with HIV/AIDS in Riverside and San Bernardino counties face everyday. "We are dealing with a virus that doesn't have a brain, but it's pretty darn smart" he said.

Benson isn't sure whether he will attend today's candlelight vigil and tree-lighting ceremony ah Koffi at the Corridor in Palm Springs. The event, one of hundreds taking place today worldwide, is hosted by the Coachella Valley-based AIDS Assistance Program, Bear Hawk Services, Desert Aids Project, Gay Associated Youth and Working Wonders.

Attending the commemoration might be too hard on the 44 year, who lost his partner of 17 years to AIDS in 2001.

"I brought him home to die in my arms," said Benson. "No one should die alone." Since then, Benson said, he leads an isolated life.

He doesn't let himself get to close to people because he couldn't live with himself if he passed along the virus. "The only reason you get infected is if you do something stupid or are ignorant of the facts" he said. He admits he was one of the stupid ones when he contracted the virus in the 1980's.

Facing the AIDS virus head on. By Stephanie Firth (continued)

He was a "functioning addict," he said, popping pills, smoking pot, shooting cocaine and methamphetamine. He went from partying with a group of 6 or 7 friends on the weekend to getting high every day after work. He shared needles. He was the first of his friends to be told he had the "Gay Plague". Now he's the last one left.

"You try and have a positive attitude'" said Benson. "But in my universe, God is a joker and I am his favorite punch line."

But lately, Benson is the one who is starting to make the jokes. He's done some stand-up comedy at the Improv in Los Angeles as well as in the Coachella Valley. He never jokes about AIDS.

The fact he's bipolar and had a troubled youth? Fair game. "I call it, 'humor from dysfunction,'" he said with a little laugh. Today Benson is sober. Clean. He's one of the Desert Aids Projects "Positive Speakers" who attend local schools to talk about drugs and AIDS.

He worries about who will take care of his two small dogs when he's gone. He worries about not working. He gets angry thinking about people who are uninformed or continue to have unprotected sex and who share needles.

He said he knows he is blessed, lucky to be alive. But sometimes he wonders why. "I see everyday as a gift," he said, picking at a loose thread on the cuff of his shirt. I don't know what's in the box but I am happy to open it everyday.

POZitively Speaking

If I had to admit what I was most proud of in this life I would have to say "Being a POZitive Speaker". I am honored that I have been able to take my story, without shame or guilt, and use it as a tool for positive change and awareness in others.

And even though I rarely ever received compensation, except for the occasional gasoline money donation, this has been more rewarding than any money could afford. And it this chapter I share the script of my POZitive speaking presentation in the hopes that it may affect some positive change is someone who reads it. I would rather share this true story in person but this script is the only means at my disposal at this time. So here it is and I hope, in some small way, it touches you and you share this story with those near and dear to you.

The Presentation

I was born in South Dakota with a Mom and Dad like most of you. I remember when I was 3 or 4 years old and Dad asked me to get him a beer.

He called me a good boy and even gave me a drink and even though it tasted good what I liked the most was the praise from my Dad. And maybe that reinforced my drinking at an early age as my Mom had left by the time I was 7 and Dad turned his anger towards us kids. I was the middle child and I felt I never got the respect I deserved. Not at home, or school and I was abused in more ways than I care to share. But that moment I felt good about myself and the reward of words and beer stuck with me as I often would steal drinks of Dad's beer and when I got older I would even take from the bar that was under our kitchen sink.

But drinking was a ways of escaping the reality of life with an alcoholic dad. Absent mother and a sister, brother and classmates that always harassed me.

So it's no wonder that by the age of 12 I was already smoking cigarettes, drinking and within a year have had my 1st joint. By the time I was 16 I had already shot up cocaine and within a year would be incarcerated and placed in reform school.

I was a high school drop out and got my G.E.D. in that place and the following year I took my SAT exams. I scored very well, in fact good enough to have been accepted at one of the best technical schools at the time, Schools of Minds and Technology in Rapid City. Not bad for a high school drop out but I didn't care for myself back then. I really didn't have any self-esteem because I had never been shown any esteem or respect growing up. My parents weren't willing to help me out but I felt they had abandoned me years before. I began running and ran for many years traveling numerous times hitch-hiking across the southern United States.

At 21 I found myself living in Palm Springs and found myself working with challenged adults. Sometimes it just seemed easier to focus on someone else's problem instead of looking at my own. But I was an addict, sure I was a successful addict. I went to work every day and partied every night and weekend. Of course this was the early 80's as instead of shooting up cocaine I was shooting up methamphetamine.

I as lucky because no one realized my secret shame until the time I missed 3 days of work in a row. I just thought I was a little fatigued. But I was required to get a doctors note which simply said I was fighting an infection. Nothing specific but enough to allow me to return to work, I returned to the doctors office 2 weeks later to find him already waiting in the exam room covered in head to toe blue gown, cap, booties and plastic mask.

I've never had a doctor ever wait for me, but there he was. I said "what's up Dr C.?" And he was like' You have that gay disease I think they are going to call HIV or AIDS. I w as in shock because I was having receptive sex. I was just a successful druggie who partied to feel better about himself and now that needing to feel good was what was going to kill me. It took 2 more years for me to quit the IV drugs and I started taking AZT. We thought it was a cure when in fact after a few short months on , what is now 2x the normal dosing, caused me to endure peripheral neuropathy. Within 6 months on AZT I had an AIDS diagnosis. That was almost 25 years ago in 1987 when I had as many friends as are in this classroom (or group).

People say I am lucky to have lived 20 plus years with this infection and still look as good as I do. But I don't think it's lucky to hold the love of your life and watch them die. I don't think it's lucky that out of 45 people I am the only one left. I don't think it's lucky that I have to carry a bag just for my medication when I travel. I don't think it's lucky that the disease and medication have affected every organ in my body. I don't think I am lucky that I got infected before we even had the proper name for this infection. I don't think it lucky that I do not have a single friend left from back then.

But I am lucky to be here in front of you. And perhaps that is the only reason why I am still alive. Alive to share my experiences, my diagnosis and this one message. If I could change anything, if I could go back to my childhood, and do something that might have made my life easier would be to find someone, anyone, to tell me this "No matter what happens, Love Yourself, Respect Yourself, Protect Yourself". Because, if I could have done anyone 1 of those things for myself I might now be here right now. And I hope you remember this "No matter what happens you can love yourself, respect yourself and protect yourself.

The Death of an Era

P.S. Make Me Laugh

Let me start off by saying that I feel blessed that I can take my life and create humor. So remember "THESE ARE JUST JOKES" even if based in my reality.

Sadly though some of this is true as well so that's why it's such a blessing to use humor to not only survive and overcome but create something better in the end. Even though this is the last section of the book that is not the reason for the title of this chapter.

In my world, in my universal faith, God has a sense of humor. You must admit that that idea would explain a lot about the state of life. And in my world every time I face a new Challenge, Dysfunction or Dysfunctional I hear God say in that quiet little voice "P.S. make Me Laugh!!!

Let's begin shall we? The sooner I start the quicker you will finish.

I heard that more than ½ of us Americans are now being raised in a Dysfunctional family. And now I hear "Before you are born you get to pick your parents." Come on...what the hell was I thinking?

Like I was up in heaven going:

"Ok God I know I'm going to find the perfect couple and there they are....right down there in the bar...yeah I want them cuz they must be rich cuz they're there a lot. Yeah God I want that fat bald alcoholic down there in the middle of the bar sitting up and passed out ! Yeah cuz he looks like he's got a great sense of balance."

"And his wife is right there dancing with my step dad...Yeah that way I get a bonus later on...I'm so happy cuz now I get 3 for the price of two.

I think a lot of people would change their 1st name if their parents could never find out. I was the only Milton born in South Dakota in nineteen hundred and sixty some years. I asked my Dad how he came up with that name. I said "where you sitting on the toilet going "Honey..what say we call it M.M.M.I.L.T.T.O.O.O.N?"

"Because I got to tell ya Dad my life has been crap ever since."

And Dad isn't the sharpest tool in the shed but I asked him again "Why Milton?" and he said "Well back then you often named kids hoping they'd grow into it. We wanted something big for you and at that time there was Milton Bradley, who made millions selling cardboard games, and Milton Bearle, who was the richest comedian at the time, of course you not very funny son, oh yeah and the biggest thing....the great Miltie Way Galaxy...nothing bigger than that. To bad you didn't live up to your name Miltie....."

P.S. make Me Laugh (continued)

It seems to me everyone has a complaint or Bitch to Pitch about their childhood. Hell some people even turn into BMW's over their childhood. That's Bitch Moan and Whine for the uniformed out there. But I grew up in South Dakota so yeah I walked 3 miles to school through 3 feet of snow…in June!!! But even before that I had to get up at 3 am to milk the cows. Come On!!! Don't they already sell this shit in the store.

One day Dad asks "What do you want for your birthday?"
And I replied "take me to the store cuz all I really want is 7 hours of sleep. But check this out Dad they got milk that not only pasteurized like we do but it's homogenized. Do you know what that means? No more lumps.

I remember one morning Dad was standing next to our biggest Holstein named Friendly slurring his speech as he said "I can't get any m-m-milk out of this cow!"
And I said "But Dad you are milking the bull…again" and I know why the damn thing lived up to it's name.

And I think our house was like every other house in South Dakota. Like underneath our kitchen sink was the comet, Windex and a full bar. I remember going "Sis what do I use to clean the dining room carpet? Comet? Windex? Charcoal filtered Vodka????
   People would come over and say "Wow it smells nice in here are you making run raisin cookies? And I reply "Nope just cleaning up a little bit of coke-a-cola I spilled on the kitchen floor.

I remember one morning Dad was furious and was like "Kids get your butts down here! Now I know one of you has been watering down the good stuff and if I find out who I'm gonna kill them !"

And my Sister was a bitch plus she was schizophrenic and not one of her "friends" liked me either. I'd hear "Well you are just a lil sissy fag with no sense of style." And I'm like "God I got no sense of style." "Jeez a fag with no style….why don't you just turn me into a bald peacock and……apparently he has. (See photo on back cover if you doubt me.)

You know I was so jealous of that crazy bitch. I was just as crazy being Bipolar but she was lucky enough that everyone could tell she was crazy.. so she got all help and drugs she needed…..plus she got friends.

I didn't have any friends in school because I went bald early. In 3rd grade everyone was like "Is he a student teacher or a Nark?"

P.S. Make Me Laugh (continued)

Speaking of bald I just looked in the mirror and thought "Oh man where did that big baby come from. Look at me – I'm bald, wide eyed and all this baby fat. The only difference is that I have more hair and less self-esteem now.

Speaking of babies I got this scar on my neck from my brother. But every thing is cool now. Only because he didn't live to tell. So here is what happened to the best of my recollection. Steve is a year younger and it was my 9th birthday and we were playing to family game Pass-Out. Steve was like so wasted and said "Here brother I got you a knife now take it" the next thing I knew I woke up bleeding and Steve was dead and Dad was there saying "That little shit I don't care what he did to you but I caught him watering down the good stuff.

Speaking of good stuff! It was so weird moving to California because I fit in. I swear Californians are just as F'd up as me except I have my papers to prove it.
"It says here you have Bipolar Affective Disorder, Reactive Attachment Disorder and Social Anxiety Disorder ! Yes sir basically I am a B.A.D., R.A.D., S.A.D Dude.

I love my mental health professionals..they are just as F'd Up as I am too. My Shrink told me one day "I should tell you I am in recovery for a pill addiction" and I said "Good then you should know how to keep me flying high huh?!"
  But then my therapist called me, which isn't the 1st time, and said "I need to reschedule because I've had a relapse" and I'm thinking "I'm Bipolar, my shrink is a pill-head, my therapist is in recovery ! You talk about the blind leading the blind.

Today was a crazy day because I had to see my Psychologist, Physciatrist, Oncologist, Gastroenterologist and got my car lubed. You know Hillary Clinton was so right when she said "It takes a village to raise our children"

I grew up early which probably explains why I'm in my 2nd childhood at 48 and look like a 5'8" tall baby. Oh how I would love to go back to those co-dependant days but who would have me.

My doctor gave me some really good news today he said "You need to loose some weight for the sake of your health…..and the health of your baby" and I said "Great now I need to go out and buy some maternity clothes"

P.S. Make Me Laugh (continued)

He laughed and said "You are so funny and so smart I wish I could be Bipolar like you" and I was thinking "Yeah like that is all that I need...a twin!" But instead I said "Doc if I am so smart how come my IQ score is 3 times higher than my 3 credit scores combined?"

Ok Doc I know you can't answer that one but tell me "was I born or made Bipolar? You know was it my nature or my Nurture" and he said "Take your pick because it's always going to be your parents fault"

So I 8-way called my family to share the good news. Actually I only called my Schizophrenic Sister. She's so cool now because she's dead. But we still talk often and today I was like "Well were getting older do you think we are going to turn into our parents?"
    And she said "Oh you don't have to worry about turning into Dad because you make such a nice drunk." And in her usual manner said" Besides don't all gay men turn into their Mothers?"
    I said "Now listen up all you bitches in there...I'm Bisexual AND Bipolar...you know...double the pleasure double the funk !" and then that little voice in my head said "Hey you liar ! You are A-Sexual you always end up dating Ass-holes" and then I said to my sister "I'm sorry I guess I'm just a little touchy since I realized I really have turned into Mom!"

I did finally finish my Christmas list only 126 days early. But it took a lot of consideration you know with the birth of the Messiah and all. Do you know what you are getting him? He's on my list...I'm giving him a loser (me) cuz it's all I can afford. And for the rest of my family :
    For Dad I'm getting the book "Who's who in American Comedy" but I know I'll have to go there and open it and say "See Dad- here I am. Milton DeWayne Benson and it says "His comedy, like his life, sucks"" and say "You see Dad I always told you I'd live up to your expectations.
    For Mom I bought the travel version of Monopoly this way we can still play when she leaves me again.
    For little brother I bought a shotgun because this year I want to be able to fire back and defend myself.
    And for my Schizo-sister, the one I was closest with, was the hardest one till I came across the book "How to Click with Everyone Every Time" Because I hope it will help the next time I have to talk to those bitches.

P.S. make Me Laugh (continued)

So after that I was feeling homesick and decided to drive around Yucca valley shich reminded me of my hometown in South Dakota. The I saw a sign for the Morongo Basin Sexual Assault Services and I stopped and ran inside and said "I'm so glad I found you because with the Holidays coming up I was feeling a little lonely and homesick and I have to admit I was abused. So I was wondering "Do you have a weekend or Holiday package? Any chance that comes with an upgrade for life?"

I have to tell you people I really that I do love California. Thanks to medicinal Marijuana I can deal with all the Dysfunction. No I don't advocate the abuse if drugs but I do advocate the sharing of drugs! So I was wondering....anyone got any chemo?

Actually I have been on chemo to save my liver. I remember there lying in bed as sick as a dog on the internet looking up the side effects of my chemo. The 1st thing listed was Murder/Suicide and all I could think was "Oh God if only I had some company!"

The second listed side effect was "May exacerbate any mental condition" so it pushed me into Bipolar Mania. But it was cool because I got to talk to God and I have to tell you people- it's so comforting to know she is bald.

I think as we get older our childhood memories get either better or worse in our minds. My childhood was just like a game show and I can hear the announcer right now. "Milton DeWayne Benson your Dad's an Alcoholic, your Mom's run away, your Sister is Schizophrenic and your Brother is stoned all day. So what are you going to do now?"

"Well I guess I'll get hooked on Dad's booze, Kim's pills, Steve's drugs and become a comic".

It turns out all my friends are worried about Identity Theft!
Me too, I'm worried about anyone that would want to be me!
Actually I don't have any friends because I don't have any money.
I mean I get these calls all the time "Hey if your going out tonight can I tag along?" and I'm like "Well that depends...what's the price on that tag? Any chance I'll get a rebate?" and they are like "Yeah right ! Get lost you loser!!!"

(Well at least now I have the time free from distraction to write this book.)
(Thanks for tagging along err reading along!)

Comedy Bio

You might wonder why someone with Social Anxiety Disorder (or is S.A.D.) and Bipolar Affective Disorder (or is B.A.D.) would be compelled to perform Stand-Up Comedy? It turns out he's a bigger Masochist whose need to be in pain outweighs his need to be in misery. Born into a life, mind and world marinated and stewed in Dysfunction he realizes this stew is best when served to as many as possible.

Come share the misery as he proves "Everything is more screwed up than I am and I'm Bipolar" and believes in Thanking God that Life SUCKS!!!!

— Epilogue —

(a brief history)

This project has been years in the working. Most of the poems where written between 2004 and 2009. The Gods of Greed written between 2006 and 2007 along with the bulk of this tome. The original concept of this book came to me shortly after my HIV/AIDS diagnosis over 20 years ago.

At that time the working title was "I looked through My Window" which will be the final piece in this small volume and was written at that time. The 2nd title was "Children of the Light" which is the opening poem. But neither title really resonated that touched on all the levels presented in this work.

Then for a short stint it lived as "P.S. make Me laugh" which ended up making an amusing title and just may be the title of my next book but I hoped you liked that chapter titled "P.S. make Me laugh". I can only hope God is still laughing!!!

Then that Divine Inspiration (Thank You God) hit me while listening to some praise songs on a Christian radio station and the title came and resonated so clearly on so many levels a tear came to my eye.

I'm am no prophet and am actually worldly enough to hope and pray that this book makes a profit. Even though I do not believe I will make a profit I hope someone else can profit from my words and somehow not only becomes more accepting of being Human but work towards being more HumanKind towards themselves and/or others.

I can only hope this book "Human Frequencies" resonates with you in some way and helps you no matter what your state of physical, mental or spiritual well-being.

I looked through My Window

I looked through my window,
What did I see?

All of the beauty given you and me.

Seeing all this greatness beyond compare,
Yet looking through life's Pain and Despair.

Learning to look at all that is around,
Realizing Happiness isn't always abound.

Looking beyond what the eyes only see,
To find the Beauty in You and Me.

Seeing also the agony, pain, anguish and sorrow,
Not to obscure a clearer tomorrow.

It's wasn't easy to see this much,
But it helps to be Honest and look with Love.
Enlightening the World so Beautifully Touched.

I look through My window,
What did I see?

As if looking in a Mirror,
I saw Me,

And in the reflection,
I was set free.

LaVergne, TN USA
30 August 2010
195051LV00002B